HOW TO DEAL WITH Gun Violence

NICK HUNTER

Published in 2026 by **Cheriton Children's Books**
1 Bank Drive West, Shrewsbury, Shropshire, SY3 9DJ, UK

First Edition

Author: Nick Hunter
Designer: Paul Myerscough
Editor: Sarah Eason
Proofreader: Nicky Hughes

Picture credits: Cover: Shutterstock/Marko Subotin.
Inside: p1: Shutterstock/Jerel Cooper, p4: Shutterstock/Vchal, p5: Shutterstock/Jamilya Khalilulina, p6: Shutterstock/Matthew Moloney, p7: Shutterstock/Whitney Welshimer, p8: Shutterstock/Jerel Cooper, p9: Shutterstock/Tiko Aramyan, p10: Shutterstock/Vic Hinterlang, p12: Shutterstock/Sandor Szmutko, p13: Shutterstock/SpeedKingz, p14: Shutterstock/Laiotz, p15: Shutterstock/Diego Cervo, p16: Shutterstock/LA Photography/Aaron, p18: Shutterstock/Txking, p19: Shutterstock/Mark Reinstein, p20: Shutterstock/Rebekah Zemansky, p21: Shutterstock/Kate Way, p22: Shutterstock/Gorodenkoff, p23: Shutterstock/Boyphare, p24: Shutterstock/New Africa, p26: Shutterstock/Trevor Bexon, p27: Shutterstock/Amee Cross, p28: Shutterstock/KMH Photovideo, p29: Shutterstock/Kate Way, p30: Shutterstock/ButtermilkgirlVirginia, p31: Shutterstock/Damann, p32: Shutterstock/JA Images, p34: Shutterstock/Traci L Clever, p35: Shutterstock/Chris Dorney, p36: Shutterstock/Brent Eysler, p37: Shutterstock/Lyonstock, p38: Shutterstock/Cass Tippit, p40: Shutterstock/Rena Schild, p41: Shutterstock/Glynnis Jones, p42: Shutterstock/KMH Photovideo, p44: Shutterstock/Ben Von Klemperer.

Printed in China

Contents

An Epidemic of Violence

Almost every day seems to bring news of another mass shooting in the United States. Since 2020, there have been more than 600 mass shootings in the country every year. And more than 50 people every day die in homicides involving guns. Gun violence has become an epidemic, claiming thousands of lives every year.

Seven out of 10 gun owners in the United States say they own a handgun.

Many Lives Lost

A mass shooting is an incident in which at least four people are shot and injured or killed. In 2017, a mass shooting in Las Vegas resulted in more than 50 fatalities and more than 500 injured people. Most incidents are much smaller, but still result in deaths and life-changing injuries for many people. The impact of these shootings then spreads in the grief and heartache experienced by family and friends of victims.

Stopping the Violence

Surveys show that eight out of 10 Americans believe that gun violence is a problem for the country. However, there are many disagreements about the best way to solve the problem.

The United States is the only country in the world where there is more than one gun for each member of the civilian population, with around 120 firearms per 100 Americans. The causes and effects of gun violence are a subject for heated political debate. Campaigners for gun control believe that many lives could be saved if the government did more to regulate the types of firearm that people can buy, and tried to carry out more checks on people who want to own guns.

A Twenty-First Century Debate

There are many questions about the best ways to deal with gun violence and the deaths and injuries it causes. People have differing views about this growing twenty-first century issue. This book looks at the facts about gun violence. It also explores some of the debates that surround this issue and its effect on both individuals and society.

Rights and Freedoms

For a lot of people, the right to own guns is an important part of American life. Many Americans are fiercely proud and protective of the freedom to bear arms, which they believe is guaranteed by the US Constitution. Supporters of gun rights argue that banning these weapons is not the way to end gun violence. They believe that a ban would restrict the basic rights of Americans.

These flowers were placed in memory of a 16-year-old victim of gun violence in Denver, Colorado.

Chapter 1

What Is Gun Violence?

When you think about gun violence, what images or situations come to mind? They may be based on what you see in the news or how gun violence is shown on television and in movies. Movies often show guns being used in battles between criminal gangs and police officers. Gun violence on television news may highlight the worst of the mass shootings that happen almost every day somewhere in the United States. These examples are just the most high-profile, well-known events involving guns. The reality of gun violence is a more complex picture.

Deaths from Firearms

Guns typically claim more than 40,000 lives every year. For every fatal shooting, there are also injuries that can range from more minor gunshot wounds to serious, life-threatening injuries leading to permanent disabilities. The number of total deaths and the number of homicides using firearms have both increased steadily since the 1990s. It is a fact that gun violence in the United States is getting worse.

Sadly, more than half of the deaths related to firearms are due to people taking their own lives. A few hundred deaths caused by firearms are classified as accidental, and a similar number are the result of police or other law enforcement. Almost half of all firearms deaths are homicides.

Police attend the scene of a shooting in Boston, Massachusetts.

Thousands of people every year are touched by gun violence, affecting them or friends and family.

Statistics Behind Homicide

Just over 20,000 people per year have been murdered using firearms in recent years. Behind this shocking figure is a complex picture. Some of these homicides are carried out by criminals and gangs. Many of these incidents are criminals fighting rival gangs. In the movies, these battles rarely impact ordinary people's lives. However, ordinary people and passersby can easily get caught up in these crimes or be targeted in armed robberies.

Truths about Terrorism

In a few cases, terrorists may target ordinary people to try to achieve a political goal, such as highlighting their extreme religious views or hatred of particular groups in society. A lot of effort is put into preventing terrorist attacks, with strong security at public events and airports. Terrorism is something that many of us worry about. However, in most years, the number of people killed in terrorist attacks is less than 100, so only a tiny percentage of all gun-related homicides are due to terrorism.

Those who carry out mass shootings may be motivated by racism or prejudice against particular groups of people.

Random Events

Other homicides appear to be more random. There are many examples of lone gunmen who attack crowded places such as workplaces, shopping malls, or colleges. These mass shootings often make headlines because they seem random, and it can be so difficult to understand why innocent people have been targeted in these shootings. The number of fatalities in this type of attack varies each year, but is normally only several hundred people so only accounts for 5 percent of all gun-related homicides. Figures from the Federal Bureau of Investigation (FBI) show that the number of "active shooter incidents" involving someone firing a gun in a populated area have increased significantly since the year 2000.

Gun Violence at Home

Most gun violence is not targeted against strangers in public places. There are more firearms than people in the United States, and this means that many homes contain a gun. Victims of homicide are often known to the attacker and may include partners and other family members. Guns in the home are also one of the reasons for the number of gun-related accidental deaths every year.

Where Does Gun Violence Happen?

We might assume that the highest rates of gun-related deaths would be in some of our largest cities, where gang violence and street crime are usually higher. This is not always true. The highest gun homicide rates are in Washington DC and southeastern states such as Mississippi, Alabama, and Louisiana. The states with the lowest rates include Massachusetts and rural states such as Idaho and Iowa.

The facts about different forms of gun violence show that it can be difficult to generalize about this complex issue. Gun violence happens for a lot of different reasons.

Domestic violence (see page 15) is often the reason for gun-related deaths within the home.

Is the United States Different?

How does the United States' experience of gun violence compare to other countries? Americans are 25 times more likely to be killed by gun homicide than people in other wealthy countries. In the United States, gun-related killings account for 80 percent of homicides. In Canada, the figure is 30 percent. In England, which has strict laws about gun ownership, the figure is just 4 percent. The US homicide rate is 7 times higher than European countries such as Germany, France, and the United Kingdom (UK). However, the gun-related homicide rate is higher in many Latin American countries such as El Salvador, Venezuela, and Guatemala.

Do People Have the Right to Bear Arms?

"A well-regulated militia, being necessary to the security of a free state, the right of the people to keep and bear arms, shall not be infringed."

These are the words of the Second Amendment to the US Constitution, passed in 1789. Supporters of gun ownership use the words to justify the idea that all Americans have the right to bear arms, or own guns. They also use them to argue that government should not try to restrict that right. Those who support more control of guns believe that the damage done by guns is unacceptable. They do not believe we should use a document written more than 200 years ago to justify it. Let's take a look at both sides of the debate.

The Right to Bear Arms

Supporters of gun rights argue that owning a gun is an American right for the following reasons:

US Constitution: The right to bear arms is included in the Bill of Rights. The Constitution and the Bill of Rights are the basis for American government and the rights of all Americans.

Most guns are used responsibly: We do not ban things just because some people use them illegally. Millions of people own guns, but only a small number of these people commit crimes.

Government interference and discrimination: Government should not interfere in people's lives by deciding whether someone can own a gun. Deciding who can own a gun discriminates against some groups of people. That is not fair.

Conclusion

All Americans have had the right to bear arms because it was written down by the country's founders. Just because some use the weapons to commit crime, that does not mean the government should remove a basic American right.

Gun Ownership Is Not a Right

Campaigners argue in favor of gun control for the following reasons:

Times change: Current gun laws are out of date because the Second Amendment was written at a time when the United States had just gained its independence from Great Britain. It states the right to bear arms as part of a "well-regulated militia" to protect the new country. It relates to the time it was written and is not relevant today.

Protecting people is most important: People do not have the right to own guns if that puts other people's lives at risk. The right to life and to safety is more important than someone's right to own a gun.

Most people want gun control: Surveys show that a majority of Americans agree that some people, such as those with a history of violence, should not be allowed to own guns. The government should make laws to protect people, rather than laws that protect gun owners.

Conclusion

The Second Amendment was written a long time ago when the United States was very different. Most people agree that we need to reduce gun violence. We should not put protecting the Constitution above keeping people safe.

What Do You Think?

After reading both sides of the argument, what conclusions do you draw? Do you think we have a right to own guns? Or do you think US laws on guns should be designed to keep people safe?

Chapter 2

What Causes Gun Violence?

Gun violence is caused by the same things that cause any other form of violence. People commit crimes for all sorts of reasons. However, if they have access to a gun, it is more likely to be used in the crime. Violence is also caused by sudden anger or arguments between people. Guns are not just used by people who intend to commit crime but are used at times of high stress and emotion.

Joining a street gang may give young people a sense of belonging, but gun violence is often part of this culture.

Gun Use and Crime

Ocala in Florida has one of the highest rates of gun crime in the United States. It ranks highly alongside other gun violence hotspots (such as St Louis, Missouri, and Detroit, Michigan) for firearms incidents and injuries. According to news reports, much of this violence is between older teenagers, with young people being targeted in apartment complexes or drive-by shootings. Campaigners say that this violence is driven by "back-and-forth beef" between groups of young people. Arguments often begin on social media and end in violence.

Gun violence is often a particular problem among teenagers and young adults in large cities. Experts believe the root cause of this may lie in poverty, poor housing, and family situations that mean young people lack opportunities and good adult role models.

Gang Violence

These factors can then lead to involvement in drug use and selling as well as street gangs, in which carrying guns and gun violence is a fact of life.

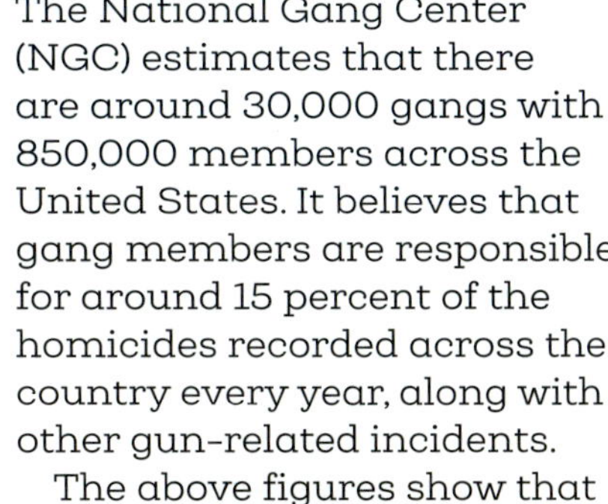

The National Gang Center (NGC) estimates that there are around 30,000 gangs with 850,000 members across the United States. It believes that gang members are responsible for around 15 percent of the homicides recorded across the country every year, along with other gun-related incidents.

The above figures show that gang membership is one of the key factors in gun violence. People join gangs for many reasons. They may even join a gang because they think it will offer protection from other gangs. However, evidence shows that gang members are much more likely to themselves be victims of gun violence, as well as being responsible for many gun crimes that are committed.

Violent gang culture is not just limited to the United States. For example, in other countries such as the UK, knife crime is a big problem among young people. This is often driven by the same factors—a lack of opportunities, drug use, and social media disputes. The key difference is that there are much tougher regulations on gun ownership in other countries, so young people are less likely to be able to use a firearm to carry out violence.

In many countries, knife crime is a bigger issue than gun crime because of tight gun laws.

Guns in Use

Handguns are the most common firearms responsible for violent crime. FBI figures show that handguns are used in around 60 percent of homicides. Rifles and shotguns combined are used in less than 5 percent. The guns used in the other 35 percent of homicides are unknown or from another category. Handguns are more easily portable, which explains why they are used so widely in gun crimes.

Unequal Impact

Where you live and who you are can make you more likely to be a victim of gun violence. Half of all gun homicides take place in major cities that are home to only one-quarter of the US population. These areas are also more likely to have a large Black population. Just over half of the victims of gun-related homicides in the United States are Black men, although they make up only 6 percent of the total population. Black men are also much more likely to be involved in firearms incidents with police officers.

Gun violence is more of a problem in inner-city areas with few jobs or other opportunities.

More than half of homicides in the home are committed with firearms.

Domestic Violence

Gun ownership in the home is linked to other crimes and violence. Domestic violence happens when one member of a family or household physically attacks other members of the family. Victims of domestic violence are much more likely to be killed if the violent person has access to a gun. Victims of domestic violence are also more likely to be women and children.

Causes of Mass Shootings

One of the biggest questions for law enforcement is to discover the reasons behind the disturbing number of mass shootings. The attackers who carry out these mass shootings may have their own particular motive for their actions, but research by the Secret Service has found some common elements in these attacks. It found that more than nine out of 10 attackers had been dealing with some type of personal problem in the time leading up to their attack. These issues included divorce, problems at school or work, and health problems. These stressful events lead some people–and almost all were men–to respond violently, using a firearm to cause harm to others.

We can see that gun-related incidents have many different causes, but does the presence of guns themselves actually make our society more dangerous?

Does Gun Ownership Make Society More Violent?

Incidents of gun-related violence have one thing in common–the gun. Campaigners against gun ownership argue that the availability of firearms in society is the biggest reason for such high rates of violence and homicide in our country. Many people disagree, arguing that law-abiding citizens are actually safer if they have a gun. Let's take a look at both sides of the debate.

Guns Are Not the Problem

Supporters of gun rights argue that guns are not the cause of more violence in society for the following reasons:

Causes of violence: Guns do not cause violence themselves. The causes lie in problems in wider society, such as gang culture and conflict over supplying illegal drugs. Life pressures such as poverty and mental illness are also linked to gun violence.

Guns for protection: Law-abiding people who own guns are more protected from violent attacks and robberies directed at themselves and their property. People would not be able to defend themselves if unarmed. Guns help those people to protect themselves and property.

Criminals will find a way: Even if there were fewer guns and tighter regulations, criminals will always find a way to illegally buy guns. For that reason, it is better if other members of society have guns too.

Conclusion

Guns make law-abiding people safer from criminals. Violence is not caused by owning a gun, it is caused instead by criminal acts. Criminals have access to guns so the rest of us need them too for protection.

Guns Make Society More Violent

Anti-gun campaigners feel that guns lead to more violence in society for the following reasons:

Increasing impact of anger and disagreement: Problems will always exist in society and cause conflict between people, but if those people have access to guns the conflict is more likely to result in someone being killed or seriously injured.

Carrying guns does not make us safer: There is evidence that owning a gun may help to protect property but it does not make a person any safer and may instead increase the chance that they will be shot.

Experience of other countries: Other countries have similar problems with violence and disagreements. However, because they have much tighter gun laws, homicide levels are mostly much lower than in the United States.

Conclusion

There is no definite evidence that guns make people safer. The key reason why the United States has much higher homicide rates than similar countries is because of the easy availability of guns.

What Do You Think?

After reading both sides of the argument, what conclusions do you draw? Do you think firearms play an important role in keeping us safe? Or do you think that guns are the main reason why the US homicide rate is so high?

Chapter 3

The Effects of Gun Violence

The most obvious effect of gun violence on individuals and society is the high number of lives needlessly lost every year because of gun-related incidents. However, gun violence has many other effects on individuals, and on wider American society.

Death and Injury

Every life lost through gun violence has direct effects on the lives of the victim's family members and friends. As well as the grief of losing a loved one, gun violence can have a far-reaching impact on the family's life if the victim is the main wage-earner in the family. Lives claimed by gun violence are much more likely to be concentrated in age groups

In some states, permitless carry laws allow people to carry guns openly on the street.

below the age of 35. These victims are likely to be young adults–brothers, sisters, and young parents–with much of their lives still ahead of them.

The human cost of gun violence does not stop with thousands of fatalities every year. For every person killed, more than two people are injured by guns, adding up to nearly 100,000 people every year. These people may suffer serious injuries that lead to permanent disability. This can have a dramatic impact on the injured victims' later life chances and medical needs.

Black Communities

Gun violence affects some areas and communities much more than others, particularly inner-city areas and young Black men. Washington DC has the highest rate of gun-related injuries, with 134 per 100,000 people every year. Rural New Hampshire only has 3 injuries per 100,000 people. In Washington DC and other cities, the rate of gun-related injuries is much higher among young Black men and within mostly Black neighborhoods. Native American and Hispanic communities also suffer more gun-related injuries than experienced by white people.

Cycle of Violence

The concentration of gun violence has a powerful effect on ethnic minority communities. It means that many families are touched by gun violence and everyone knows people who have been killed and injured. Gun violence has become a huge problem in these communities because of poverty and lack of opportunity, which help gangs to recruit new members. Gun violence makes it even more difficult to overcome these problems as few people want to start businesses and bring jobs to violent neighborhoods.

Police investigate a murder scene in Washington DC, which has one of the highest rates of gun violence in the country.

Guns and Young People

Gun violence in inner-city neighborhoods has the biggest effect on younger men and teenagers. Nearly 80 percent of young people who are shot survive, but their experience can affect them and require medical care for many years. Even if they are not directly involved in gun violence, young people often see or experience gun violence in the community.

Experiencing Trauma and Mental Health Issues

Gun-related injuries can have a serious impact on the physical and mental health of victims and their families. Physical injuries vary. Damage to the spine can lead to long-term paralysis, so the victim has to use a wheelchair. Head injuries can lead to loss of memory and other damage to the brain that has a serious long-term effect on the victim's life.

As well as physical pain, victims of gun violence are more likely to seek help and medication for mental illness. Drug and substance abuse also rises among these victims. As well as victims themselves, their parents, brothers, and sisters often experience more physical and mental health problems. Young people who experience gun violence often have problems in their education, including missing school and not being able to concentrate on their studies.

These victims of gun violence are campaigning for more background checks on people buying firearms.

School employees take part in an active shooter drill.

Community Trauma

Gun violence leads to trauma and mental health issues right across a community. Shootings and armed crime in places such as stores, workplaces, places of worship, schools, and other public places make people feel unsafe. This may affect whether they are comfortable going out to work, school, or to stores.

Painful Effects of Mass Shootings

Mass shootings are often the most visible element of gun violence in the United States. They feature in news reports and often lead to politicians promising action to cut gun crime. Mass shootings are horrific and scary events, but they only make up a small part of deaths and injuries from gun violence in the United States. Mass shooting can have a big impact on people's fear of gun violence. Taking precautions, such as regular active shooter drills in schools can affect students' and parents' mental well-being and anxiety about gun violence. Some people also question whether these drills are effective in saving lives.

Young Victims of Gun Violence

For many years, motor vehicle accidents were the main cause of death for children and young people in the United States. Policymakers and governments have focused on passing measures to make our roads safer. Partly as a result of this, in 2020, firearms overtook vehicle accidents as the leading cause of death for people aged 18 and under.

Dealing with the effects of gun violence are a major issue for paramedics, and increase the risks for these lifesavers.

Economic Impact

Gun violence also has a big economic cost across the United States. One estimate put the cost of gun crime at a massive $557 billion in 2024. At almost $1,700 for every person in the United States, this sounds like a huge figure. However, the great costs of gun violence are felt across society.

Healthcare Costs

The immediate costs of gun violence are the increased healthcare costs to treat more than 100,000 injuries, and resulting deaths, every year. Each fatal shooting costs thousands of dollars in doctors' time and other medical expenses. However, costs of injuries can be much higher as a victim may need further care for many years following the incident because of the physical and mental effects of a shooting.

The Justice System

Another service on the front line of dealing with gun violence is police and law enforcement. Every year, police officers are killed and injured dealing with gun crime. Gun violence also takes up a huge amount of police time. People responsible for gun violence are then dealt with by courts and the legal system, and are likely to spend many years in prison. Across the United States, around 2 million people are in prison, costing the country many billions of dollars to keep them there. Many of those prisoners committed gun crimes.

Effects of Gun Crime on Policing

With such high levels of gun violence, police officers must assume that most suspected criminals are armed. This makes police more likely to use firearms themselves in the name of self-defence or if they believe that others are in danger. Hundreds of people are shot and killed by police each year. While many of these fatalities are armed and dangerous people, campaigners argue that some of these victims are later found to be unarmed. Arguments that the police are too quick to use guns, or that fatalities are higher in some communities, have led people to lose trust in the police. This has triggered protests such as the Black Lives Matter (BLM) movement, protesting inequality and unfair treatment of Black Americans.

Quality of Life

Other costs of gun violence include the costs to businesses. These can be due to absence or replacing employees who are killed and injured. There may also be costs in protecting businesses from gun crime directly. There is also a high cost to society in lost quality of life. Every life cut short means a lost contribution to society. It could also mean a loss to the quality of life for a family and a wider group of friends.

The effects of gun violence on our society are serious and far-reaching. Can the level of gun ownership in the United States be justified, and what can be done to reduce gun violence?

Use of firearms by police is often controversial and affects relationships with the police in many communities.

21ST CENTURY DEBATES

Is Use of Guns Ever Justified?

Gun violence clearly has a big impact on society as thousands of people are killed or injured every year. Most of this violence is linked to crime or deliberate homicide. However, if we support the right for people to own guns, are there times when it is justifiable to use guns? Some argue this is the case, while others believe we would be better off without any guns at all. Let's explore the two arguments.

Gun Use Can Be Justified

Supporters of gun ownership argue that gun use can be justified for the following reasons:

Self-defence: The only defence against a bad guy with a gun is a good guy with a gun. Owning and using a gun is justified if you are threatened by someone else who plans to attack you with a gun.

Deterring crime: The best way to deal with crime is to stop it from happening. If criminals expect that people have guns, they are less likely to take the risk of committing crime. That is because it could lead to their own injury or death if their victim has a gun too.

Law enforcement: In a society in which most criminals have guns, law enforcement need to be able to protect themselves and others. This is clearly justifiable when facing an armed criminal.

Conclusion

Supporters of the right to use guns argue that criminals have guns so others need to have guns to protect themselves and to make criminals think twice before committing crime. This also applies to police and others who need to protect the public. They need guns for safety.

Gun Use Cannot Be Justified

Opponents of gun ownership argue that owning and using guns is wrong for the following reasons:

Unsafe self-defence: Most people are not confident enough to use a gun for self-defence. This could lead to dangerous accidents or unnecessary violence in a crime situation, which actually puts people in more danger.

Guns do not make us safer: Widespread gun ownership does not deter crime. Instead, criminals know they stand the risk of being shot and this makes them more likely to carry a gun and to use it.

Human rights: The most basic human right is the right to life. Using guns for self-defence or by police may lead to the death of innocent people or those who are responsible for minor crimes. That does not represent justice.

Conclusion

More guns do not make people safer. They lead to accidents, and criminals are more likely to use firearms if they believe other people will. There are many examples every year of innocent people being killed simply because someone mistakenly fired a gun at them.

What Do You Think?

After reading both sides of the argument, what conclusions do you draw? Do you think that guns are the best way to protect ourselves from criminals? Or do you feel there is no justification for owning or using a gun?

Chapter 4

Dealing with Gun Violence

Gun violence has negative effects across our entire society, from the lives cut short and people living with terrible injuries to the neighborhoods taken over by criminal gangs. Dealing with the effects of gun violence involves many stages, from treating the injured to deciding who should be allowed to own a gun. How do people go about dealing with the effects of gun violence and reducing its impact?

A Public Health Issue

Doctors and other health professionals are on the front line of dealing with the effects of gun violence. Emergency medical services or paramedics arriving on the scene of a shooting must quickly establish what a victim's injuries are and how serious they may be. Treating gunshot wounds is a daily issue for hospital staff.

Understanding Gun Violence

As with any other health issues, health professionals are constantly trying to understand the causes of gun violence and trying to find more effective ways to treat victims. Data from emergency services can help to pinpoint the places where gun violence is a bigger issue. Unlike many other health issues, such as a number of diseases, gun violence most

For many people, tighter laws on gun ownership is the main way to deal with gun-related deaths.

Many people believe that exposing children to gun culture will lead to future gun problems.

greatly affects younger people. It is also more likely to affect young Black men than other members of the community. Training other community members in first aid can be an important step to ensure victims get the help they need as quickly as possible.

Health professionals also try to prevent gun violence by identifying those people who are most likely to be using guns. For example, young men who are injured by guns are more likely to carry out gun violence in future. Healthcare services can provide counseling or help with finding jobs. These programs can take people away from the crime and gang culture that is part of gun violence, and maybe end the cycle of violence.

Gun Safety

Public health workers also stress the importance of education in gun safety in reducing injuries and deaths. Gun safety programs include guidance on secure storage and how to handle guns safely. Many gun control campaigners believe that gun safety training should be mandatory before someone can buy a gun.

Storing guns both safely and securely can prevent accidents or guns getting into the hands of the wrong people. Officials now estimate that more than 4 million children live in a home with at least one unsecured gun, and many more children may visit homes like this.

Never Again

In February 2018, a gunman attacked a high school in Parkland, Florida. He killed 17 students and injured many more. This deadly event changed the lives of hundreds of students and their families. Within a few days, the students started a campaign to try and ensure that no other school would have to go through the same thing. The students took on politicians and lobby groups such as the National Rifle Association (NRA), calling for more checks on people buying guns. They encouraged students across the country to join the protests. The Parkland students were able to achieve real change, such as raising the legal age for buying guns in Florida.

Preventing Mass Shootings

When mass shootings take place, this normally puts the spotlight on the best ways to avoid these tragedies. While many public locations such as airports are protected by security, these incidents often take place in locations such as workplaces or schools, which are not normally protected by the same level of security.

School Security

There are many solutions suggested to the problem of security in public places. Most people agree that it is important to stop guns or people who intend to do harm

A crowd demands tougher gun laws in Florida, including students affected by the Parkland school shooting.

Tougher security can play a role in cutting the risk of school shootings.

from being able to access public buildings such as schools. Many schools have introduced metal detectors, cameras, and security guards to improve security.

Some supporters of gun rights argue that "the best way to stop a bad guy with a gun is a good guy with a gun." These people believe that gun violence can be deterred by more people carrying guns, including schoolteachers. They argue that first responders can never arrive at a scene quickly enough to prevent shootings. In many areas, schools prefer to remain gun-free but in some states, staff are allowed to carry guns.

Opponents of arming school staff argue that doing so will damage trust between teachers and students. They also point out that armed school staff have failed to stop mass shootings in the past. Armed staff can also create confusion for first responders trying to deal with an emergency.

Deterring Gun Crime

Police normally only get involved in dealing with gun violence once a crime has taken place and the damage has been done. The threat of arrest and going to jail is designed to deter people from committing a crime. Existing laws can be used to cut gun crime. They include ensuring that current laws are followed or giving tougher penalties for minor breaches of gun laws. Police can also work with local communities and increase patrols in areas with high levels of gun violence.

Gun Control

When the media and politicians talk about the best ways to deal with gun violence, most of the focus is on gun control. This can mean controlling who can buy or own guns. It also includes restricting the types of weapon people buy, so the most powerful and dangerous firearms do not make their way onto the streets.

The idea of gun control is that more guns lead to more gun violence, so if we can cut sales of guns there will be fewer deaths and injuries. However, not everyone agrees with this argument. Many states allow gun owners to carry firearms in public places, either openly or concealed. Research studies have been carried out to compare homicides before and after these laws were passed. They found that the right-to-carry laws reduce homicides. Other research shows that areas with tougher laws about who can buy guns have lower rates of gun violence.

Background Checks

The aim of those calling for more gun control is to keep guns away from people who will use them for crime or violence. Many experts believe better background checks for people buying guns would be helpful in reducing violence. People convicted of gun violence often have a prior criminal record. Gun violence is also often linked to mental illness or negative life experiences. Background checks can identify gun buyers who may present a risk.

Restricting who can buy guns may only be a part of the solution, and there are more than 300 million guns already in use in the United States. Guns can be transferred between individuals without many of the usual checks that businesses have to make. There are many ways for someone who wants a gun to get one.

Many Americans are strongly opposed to tighter controls on owning guns.

A gun show in Oklahoma, offering thousands of weapons for sale.

Assault Weapons

Some guns are more dangerous than others. Assault weapons are capable of firing more bullets at higher speeds than other rifles and handguns. Each shot from these powerful guns also does greater damage to the human body. These dangerous weapons have been used in many mass shootings, and can lead to more casualties than other firearms. Some states have banned these weapons. However, campaigners believe that wider bans would help to reduce deaths and injuries that result from gun violence.

Some of the gun-control measures introduced seem to be effective, such as more police patrols in gun-violence hotspots. However, levels of gun violence have risen since the 1990s and are affected by many factors, including economic conditions and unemployment. Many measures have only been tried in some parts of the country. Debates over how to cut gun violence remain fierce between different political groups. Republicans and Americans living outside major cities tend to be more in favor of gun ownership.

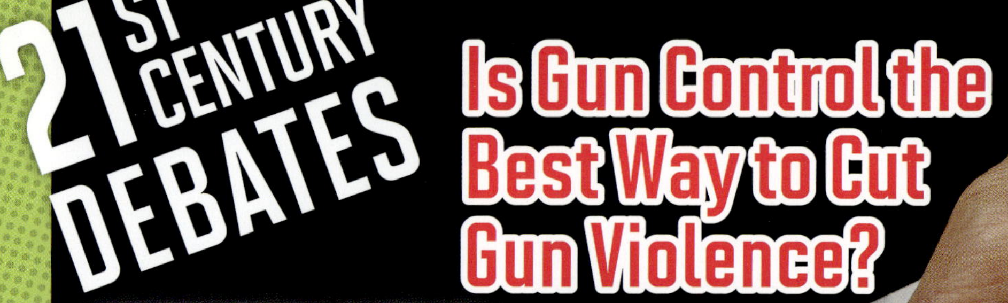

Is Gun Control the Best Way to Cut Gun Violence?

The United States is sharply divided about the issue of gun control and whether more restrictions on guns would reduce gun crime. Anti-gun campaigners argue that other measures will not work without laws to control the sale of guns. Believers in gun rights say that there is little evidence to support this argument and there are many other issues to consider. Here are both arguments.

Gun Control Will Work

Campaigners believe gun control is the best way to reduce gun violence for the following reasons:

Fewer guns mean fewer homicides: European countries have far fewer homicides than the United States. This is not because they are more united and less violent than the United States. It is because they have tough gun laws. Knife crime is often a problem in these countries, but someone armed with a knife is usually less dangerous than the same person armed with a gun.

More checks to reduce risks: More background checks on who can buy guns will stop guns going to known criminals or people who are more likely to misuse them. That will help control gun ownership.

Less dangerous weapons: Bans on more powerful weapons such as assault rifles will save lives, but people will still be able to own guns if they want to. Bans will not work.

Conclusion

Gun control is the best option to reduce gun violence. That is because it will result in fewer guns on the streets. Authorities will also have more control over who has access to guns. The United States has more guns than most other countries and this is a major reason why there is more gun violence.

Gun Control Is Not the Answer

Opponents of gun control argue that it is not the best way to reduce gun violence for these reasons:

Fewer guns may not make us safer: Research studies have not shown enough clear evidence that gun control reduces the number of gun-related homicides. Many owners of guns buy firearms for self-defence, which may even reduce the level of gun violence.

Tackling causes of gun violence: Healthcare professionals focus on other measures to reduce the amount and impact of gun crime. Gun violence is worst in inner-city communities with high unemployment and few opportunities. It is more effective to tackle causes of violence rather than banning guns.

Dealing with existing guns: Even if most new gun sales stopped, there are already more guns than people in the United States. These guns can be bought and sold by individuals without the same checks that people must go through to be able to buy new weapons.

Conclusion

Gun control will not work as it is only tackling a small part of the problem—the sale of new guns and who can buy them. Instead, authorities need to look at the causes of gun crime and neighborhoods where this is a big problem, and educate people about owning guns responsibly.

What Do You Think?

After reading both sides of the argument, what conclusions do you draw? Do you think that gun control will be the solution to gun violence? Or do you think the problem is more complex and controlling sales of guns is not dealing with the most important issues?

Chapter 5

Guns, Politics, and Society

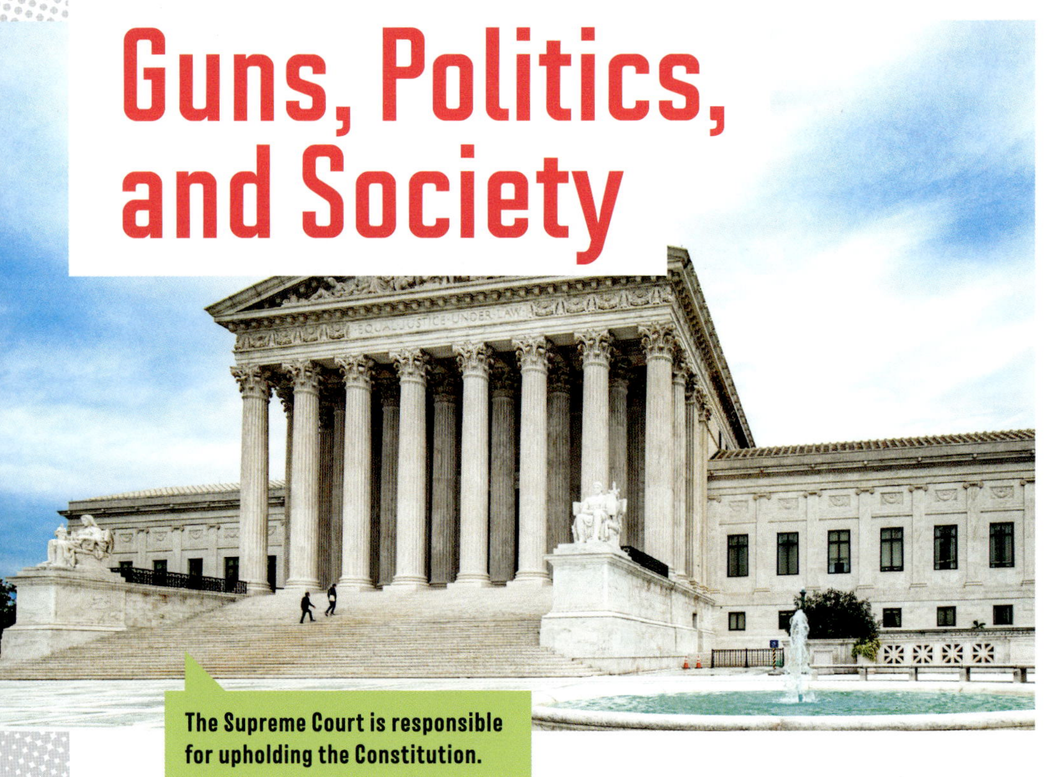

The Supreme Court is responsible for upholding the Constitution.

Whenever lives are tragically lost in another mass shooting, representatives of both Democratic and Republican political parties send their thoughts and prayers to the communities affected. Often, they pledge to pass laws or make changes to ensure that such a tragedy will never happen again. But tragedies do keep happening, and deaths from gun violence have continued to increase in recent years. Why have politicians not been able to solve this problem and what more could they do?

Passing Legislation

In 2022, an important law was passed. The Bipartisan Safer Communities Act was the most important legislation about gun violence for decades. The law included expanded background checks for those wishing to buy guns. It also closed some of the loopholes that enabled buyers and sellers of guns to avoid such checks. It put in place harsh penalties for anyone buying a gun in place of someone who would not pass background checks. The Act also put more emphasis on school safety and mental health support.

As with many aspects of gun control legislation, the Bipartisan Safer Communities Act was soon challenged in court by supporters of gun rights. Opponents claimed that it would take away Americans' right to bear arms. Republican Senators have also blocked legislation to ban assault weapons and background checks for all gun owners. Meanwhile, gun-related deaths and injuries continuc to rise.

The Supreme Court and the Second Amendment

When politicians reject gun control laws, they often refer to the US Constitution and the right to bear arms. Federal and state laws have been challenged in the courts, including the Supreme Court. The Supreme Court has ruled that people have the right to keep handguns in the home for self-defence. However, it has also stated that the right is not unlimited. Laws can be passed to stop dangerous people owning guns. They can also be passed to ban guns in sensitive places such as schools or government buildings.

The National Rifle Association (NRA)

The NRA was formed in the 1800s and is one of the most powerful voices against gun control. The organization and its millions of members argue that more guns make Americans safer. The NRA provides funding to politicians who support its views. It grades members of Congress based on how friendly they are to gun rights. The votes of the NRA's supporters can make a difference in elections. For that reason, many politicians are reluctant to criticize the NRA as it could mean losing their funding or even their jobs.

The NRA is a powerful voice in support of gun ownership.

The Firearms Industry

Debates about gun violence often focus on people who misuse guns as the cause of the problem. However, there are other players at work. The manufacture and sale of guns to Americans is big business, with more than 8 million new guns made and sold every year. Critics say that there is little attempt to control the actions of gun companies and the products they sell, which could include more safety features and checks on who buys gun products.

Public Opinion

Politicians often seem to be out-of-step with the views of most Americans. A large majority of the people believe that gun violence is a problem for the country. However, people are much more divided on how to fix the problem, with around half of Americans believing that gun ownership does more to increase people's safety. More than half of people surveyed believe gun laws should be stricter. That includes increasing the minimum age for owning a gun and stopping sales of guns to people with mental illnesses.

People in cities such as New York City are more likely to support gun control.

Protesters in Montana support the right to bear arms.

State by State

In general, there are some sharp differences between Democrats and Republicans over the place of guns in society and what responsibility the Federal Government has in taking measures to control gun crime. This issue is further complicated by the fact that some states have passed gun control measures, while other states have relaxed gun laws.

Although public opinion across the United States supports more gun control, this is often not the case in more rural states that traditionally elect Republican politicians. In Florida, a state with high levels of gun crime in many areas, some politicians have campaigned for looser gun laws. They argue that in areas of high crime it is important that the people there are able to properly defend themselves, and that law-abiding citizens have the right to own guns.

Limits of Legislation

There are limits to what legislation can achieve. Restricting who can buy firearms and types of new weapons sold will do nothing to cut the number of weapons already in use. Those guns can easily find their way to criminals and others responsible for gun violence. Gun-control campaigners are also worried that gun control laws are not keeping up with technological change. Changes in technology such as the availability of three-dimensional (3-D) printing along with homemade guns sold online mean people can avoid gun-ownership rules.

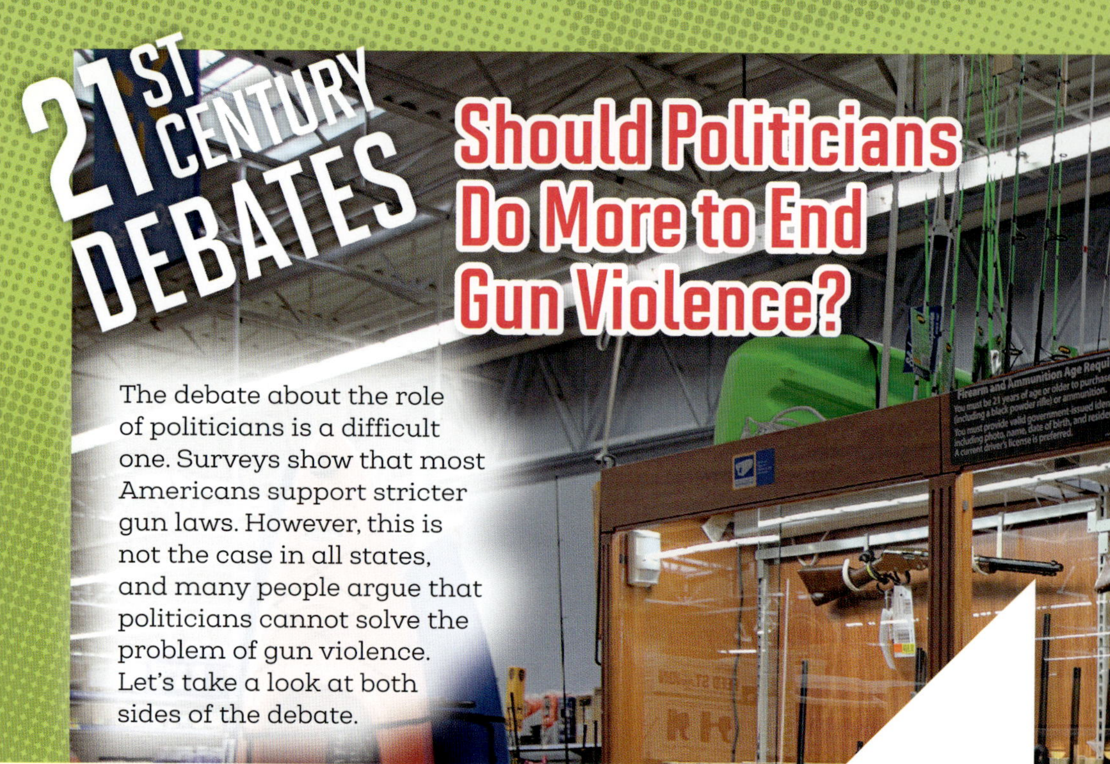

21ST CENTURY DEBATES

Should Politicians Do More to End Gun Violence?

The debate about the role of politicians is a difficult one. Surveys show that most Americans support stricter gun laws. However, this is not the case in all states, and many people argue that politicians cannot solve the problem of gun violence. Let's take a look at both sides of the debate.

Politicians Should Act

Campaigners say politicians should take the lead in cracking down on gun violence for the following reasons:

Public opinion: Eight out of 10 Americans believe gun violence is a problem for the country. A majority of people also believe there should be stricter gun laws. In a democracy, politicians should respect what people want.

Legislation is the only solution: Unless laws are passed, the gun industry will not regulate itself to stop guns reaching dangerous people. Only government can act to prevent more deaths from gun violence.

Duty to protect: The government and all politicians have a duty to protect Americans. If a foreign army or a new disease was killing 40,000 Americans every year, politicians would act immediately. Why do they not take the same approach to gun violence?

Conclusion

There have been consistent calls for gun control laws to be passed, and protecting people from harm should be a basic duty of every politician at state or federal level. Gun violence continues to increase and more legislation is the only way to stop this escalation.

Politicians Do Not Need to Take Action

Gun rights campaigners oppose more laws to prevent gun violence for the following reasons:

Politicians reflect what voters want: Politicians need to reflect the views of people who elected them, and there are many people in some states and regions who do not support more gun control laws. Many Republican politicians make clear that they oppose legislation, and people vote for them on this basis.

There are already enough laws: Laws such as the Bipartisan Safer Communities Act have been passed to deal with gun violence. If these laws have not reduced gun violence, more laws are not the answer.

Laws will not take guns off the street: Laws focus on the sale of new guns, but there are already millions of guns around the country. Criminals can get hold of guns even if they can't buy them legally.

Conclusion

Without changing the Constitution, politicians are limited in what they can do. Making changes may also not be popular with the people who elected them. Many of the guns already used by criminals would be illegal under current laws and these laws have not been successful in reducing gun violence.

What Do You Think?

After reading both sides of the argument, what conclusions do you draw? Do you think that politicians' lack of action has led to the epidemic of gun violence? Or do you think there is not a lot that politicians can do and the existing laws are good enough?

Chapter 6

Gun Violence Solutions

The problem of gun violence is a complex one with many different causes. This is one reason why it is so difficult to solve. Although the number of deaths from gun violence change each year, they have risen steadily in recent years. There are now more guns in civilian homes and neighborhoods than ever before. Many campaigners are urgently trying to find a solution to prevent more lives being cut short or ruined by gun violence.

Gun Control Laws

We have seen that lawmakers are divided over the best ways to end gun violence, and whether gun control is the best approach. There has been progress in some areas, such as extending background checks for people buying guns. Other pieces of legislation have not been accepted, such as attempts to ban more powerful weapons across the United States. And when laws have been tested by the Supreme Court, they have always supported the right of all Americans to bear arms.

In the past, the Supreme Court has supported the right to bear arms, which has made things more difficult for those who want more gun control.

Sixty percent of young Americans believe that there should be tighter controls on gun ownership.

Causes of Gun Violence

Controlling who can buy guns is not the only way to reduce gun violence, especially as gun ownership is already so widespread. Many communities now focus on addressing the causes of gun violence, such as young people in inner-city neighborhoods getting involved in crime or gang culture. This can mean helping with inequality or providing unemployment so people have more opportunities in life.

Education about the dangers of guns and gun safety is another important way of dealing with this issue. Healthcare professionals try to treat gun violence like any other health issue. As well as addressing the causes, this also involves understanding how gun violence spreads in particular locations. There is hope that new technology and artificial intelligence (AI) may be able to help in tracking data on gun violence, just as it can with other epidemics.

Young Campaigners

The protest actions of young campaigners gives hope that there is a growing movement of young people who want to make a real difference to this issue. Students Demand Action is one organization that brings together groups around the country to make their voices heard. Gun violence is the biggest cause of death among young people, so your generation have the most to gain by finding solutions. The big question is whether young people can make progress when previous generations have failed to do.

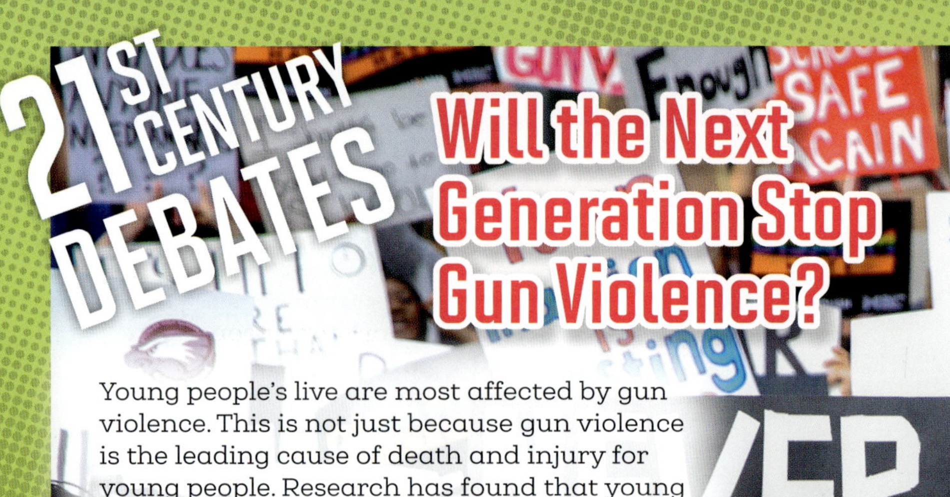

21ST CENTURY DEBATES

Will the Next Generation Stop Gun Violence?

Young people's live are most affected by gun violence. This is not just because gun violence is the leading cause of death and injury for young people. Research has found that young people have feelings of anxiety, grief, and loss about gun violence, even if they have not been directly involved in it. Does this mean that young Americans have the motivation and the commitment to solve the problem more effectively than previous generations? Let's take a look at both sides of the debate.

Young People Can End Gun Violence

Many people are optimistic about the future and believe that young Americans can make a difference for the following reasons:

Younger people have most to gain: Gun violence has the biggest impact on young people, whether in inner-city violence that particularly affects young Black men or the fear of random mass shootings. For this reason, young people have most to gain from finding solutions.

Committed campaigners: Young people have shown they can be committed campaigners for a better future on this issue. Many campaign groups that have been most effective have formed as a response to shocking tragedies such as school shootings.

Using new technology: AI and other new technologies may offer better ways of understanding the causes and patterns of gun violence. That will enable police and healthcare teams to prevent and treat gun violence more effectively.

Conclusion

Young campaigners have already shown that they can bring a fresh approach to the problem. They also have the most to gain from trying to make progress with solving it. New technology and techniques may be able to help with this.

Young People Will Not Solve the Issue

Those who are less optimistic about the issue give the following reasons:

Gun violence among the young: For all the people campaigning to end gun violence, there are many young people being sucked into crime and gang culture. That is often because they don't feel they have any other opportunities. Crime and gun violence may give these people a feeling that they are part of something, in spite of the risks.

Fierce opposition to gun control: Not everyone believes gun control is the way to solve this issue, including many young people. Those who do believe in gun control face powerful opposition from politicians and opponents of gun control, often funded by organizations such as the NRA.

The problem is too big: Gun violence is not a new problem that's easy to solve. For many people, gun violence has become a normal part of society. Many generations have failed to find a solution; why should the next generation be different?

Conclusion

Campaigning about gun violence and raising awareness about it are inspiring, but gun violence is a massive problem with many complex causes. The right to own guns is part of the US Constitution and it will take more than social media campaigns to make such a huge change to the Constitution.

What Do You Think?

After reading both sides of the argument, what conclusions do you draw? Do you believe the younger generation will find a solution to gun violence? Or do you think gun violence is just a normal part of life?

Looking for Solutions

Around half of American adults say they have had some experience with firearms. The most common experiences are being threatened with a gun or knowing a family member who was killed by a gun (including by suicide). Even if you have not had direct experience of guns, it is likely that you have taken part in an active shooter drill or know of neighborhoods where gun violence is a problem.

Try to think about how your own life has been affected by gun violence or could be affected in the future. Consider your own attitudes to some of the questions raised in this book, for example:

- Why is there so much gun violence in the United States?
- How does the risk of gun violence affect your life?
- Should Americans have the right to bear arms?
- Do you think widespread ownership of guns increases or reduces gun violence?
- What do you think would be the most effective ways to end gun violence?

Questions for Us All

You can probably think of many other questions to ask. Asking them will help you understand the issues around gun violence and how it affects your life. By understanding the issues and debates around gun violence, we will have a better understanding of why it is such a difficult problem to solve. If we all do that, we may be able to better solve some of the questions around this twenty-first century issue.

Do you think protests are effective in educating people about gun violence and changing views on this issue?

Find Out More

Books

Doeden, Matt. *Gun Violence: Fighting for Our Lives and Our Rights*. Twenty-first Century Books, 2020.

Eason, Sarah and Karen Latchana Kenney. *Being in a Gang: Stories from Survivors* (It Happened to Me). Cheriton Children's Books, 2022.

Rebman, Nick. *Gun Laws in America* (Focus on Current Events). North Star Editions, 2023.

Smith, Elliott. *Gun Violence and the Fight for Public Safety* (Read Woke Books). Lerner Publishing Group, 2022.

Websites

Everytown for Gun Safety aims to end gun violence in the United States. This page addresses some of the myths about gun violence:
www.everytown.org/debunking-gun-myths-at-the-dinner-table

Members of the NRA make their case for why they believe gun control does not work at the following site:
www.nraila.org/why-gun-control-doesn-t-work

This MSNBC news item looks at some of the causes behind gun violence, including the experience of Black Americans. Be aware that this report includes details of gun violence incidents, including in schools:
https://youtu.be/n1JpnLJBB98

Publisher's note to educators and parents:
All the websites featured above have been carefully reviewed to ensure that they are suitable for students. However, many websites change often, and we cannot guarantee that a site's future contents will continue to meet our high standards of educational value. Please be advised that students should be closely monitored whenever they access the Internet.

Glossary

active shooter drill training for members of a workplace or school so they know how to respond if they have to react to gun violence

amendment a change or modification

artificial intelligence (AI) complex computing systems in which a computer appears able to think independently, and in a similar way to a human brain

assault weapons powerful firearms designed for rapid fire and use in combat

background checks investigations into the background of a person to see if they have done anything that would make them an unfit person to buy a gun

Bill of Rights a document that is part of the US Constitution and sets out a number of basic rights of Americans

civilian someone who is not part of the armed forces

concentrated when something is packed into a small area

Constitution a document that sets out the rules followed by the US Government

criminal record an official record that shows if someone has been arrested or has committed a crime

discriminates treats a person or group of people unfairly, especially if this is due to race, religion, gender, or disability

domestic violence aggression or violent behavior in the home, such as between one member and other members of the household

drive-by shootings shootings carried out when a gun is fired from a moving car

drug and substance abuse nonmedical use of drugs or other substances, which is often illegal and may lead to issues such as addiction

epidemic the widespread outbreak of a disease, or a term used to describe something harmful that affects a lot of people

escalation increasing rapidly

fatal describes something that leads to death

fatalities deaths caused by accident or violence

Federal relating to the overall government of the United States, rather than an individual state

first responders people whose job involves being first on the scene of an emergency, such as a police officer or paramedic

gun control beliefs or laws designed to restrict access to guns or certain types of guns

gun rights beliefs that bearing arms or ownership of firearms are rights that should not be restricted

homicides killings of person carried out by other people

inequality when something is unequal, such as inequality between certain groups of people in society

interference getting involved in an issue that is not your business

justice system the system a society uses to enforce laws, including courts and prisons

law-abiding describes people who do not commit crimes or break the law

legislation a collective word for laws, as in legislation passed by Congress

majority the greater part or more than half of something

mandatory compulsory or required

mass shooting officially, an armed attack that involves death or injury for four or more people but could describe any attack affecting a large number of people

mental health relating to the health of the brain and emotional well-being

National Rifle Association (NRA) an organization that seeks to promote and campaign for the rights and views of gun owners

paralysis inability to move or feel anything in part of the body, often because of illness or injury

paramedics first responders whose job is to treat illness or injury where they happen before transferring a patient to the hospital

poverty a state of being poor or lacking something

public opinion views shared by a lot of the public

quality of life a standard of health and happiness experienced by an individual or group of people

regulate to introduce and follow rules to manage something

right moral or legal entitlement that people have and that should not be taken away

role models people who act as examples to be followed

Second Amendment amendment to the US Constitution stating that citizens have the right to bear arms

stress a state of worry or mental tension

Supreme Court the judicial branch of the US Government that rules on issues that relate to the law and the US Constitution

trauma experiencing very stressful or frightening events that we cannot control, which can affect physical and mental health

unemployment a state of being without a job

Index

About the Author

Nick Hunter is a well-known children's book author who has written books on a huge range of subjects, from history and science through politics and geography. Researching and writing this book has helped him understand the numerous and complicated issues surrounding gun crime, the risks it poses to society, and the urgent need to address this twenty-first century problem.